7.9 BILLION SHADES OF WORLD !

By

KANCHAN PRAMOD

ISBN
© Kanchan Pramod 2022

Published in India 2022 by Pencil

A brand of
One Point Six Technologies Pvt. Ltd.
123, Building J2, Shram Seva Premises,
Wadala Truck Terminal, Wadala (E)
Mumbai 400022, Maharashtra, INDIA
E connect@thepencilapp.com
W www.thepencilapp.com

DISCLAIMER: *This is a work of fiction. Names, characters, places, events and incidents are the products of the author's imagination. The opinions expressed in this book do not seek to reflect the views of the Publisher.*

DEDICATED TO,

All the different shades of this world,
my dear EARTH MATES

AUTHOR

KANCHAN PRAMOD PATEL

INDIAN AUTHOR AND POET

Connect with the author at -

kanchanpramodpatel@gmail.com

kanchanpramodd

CONTENT

LETTER - 1

(Our shades of World)

"And darling, world is exactly

how you think it is,

as ugly as you see it is

and as beautiful as you didn't knew it is,

as heartless as it sometimes is

and as kind as you didn't notice it always is,

it is as vast as an eternal ocean

and is as confined as a heart once broken,

it is as bright as a northern star

and is as dark as any never fading scar!

Dear,

World is as worst as it is

and is as best as it is,

it's a curse

it's a bliss,

because darling, the world is exactly

how you think it is,

not a bit more, nor a bit less."

Dear EARTH MATES,

Just like everything else in the world, this world itself is subjective. It is different for different people.

It can never be the same for a kid who gets all his wishes fulfilled at once and for another who barely gets any chance to wish.

This world can never seem kind to someone who lost his entire family in a tsunami. But this same world can never ever seem cruel to someone whose all family members were rescued in that same tsunami.

> *I see the reflection above water*
>
> *you see the life underneath that blue,*
>
> *both of our vision partially wrong,*
>
> *both of our vision equally true.*
>
> *Mine makes me, me.*
>
> *Yours makes you, you.*
>
> *And combined that makes us two!*

Here you see, dear EARTH MATE,
We inspite seeing the same things
don't see the same things
and that's where our worlds begin to differ.

That's where our worlds form life of

different prayers and different sins

different seasons and different springs

And at last, a life of

different losses and different wins.

For warriors, this world is a battleground,
full of enemies, hidden traps and extreme
uncertainties

For dreamers, this world is a dreamland,
full of magic, miracles and infinite hope.

And for lost ones, dear EARTH MATE,
this world is a maze, full of twists and turns
and infinite roads branched in different
directions but ultimately leading to one same
place. For them it is a never ending saga of pain,
sufferings and helplessness.

Earth dust has it all

buried underneath its layers,

the blood of mighty warriors

and the devotion of passionate lovers,

the never ending dilemma of lost wanderers

And the incomplete desires of all those sufferers!

Ask people around you what do they think of
this world and you'll see,
**every other person's idea of this world is
different,**
the way they see this world is different
and what they expect from this world is
different.

But in the end,
A happy life is all we crave.

> *The fly buzzing near your ear*
>
> *can make you happy,*
>
> *even the blank page of a book*
>
> *can make you giggle too,*
>
> *the delight roams all around*
>
> *but the one to choose it has to be you!*

Celebrate small reasons of happiness
And happiness shall never leave you deficient of
reasons to celebrate.

And though everyone's definition of this world is different, everyone's definition is correct. Since our perspective towards the world depends upon our past experiences, struggles and circumstances.

So its really okay for your idea of world to be different than someone else's idea of world, since you two may not have faced the same society, the same past and the same tragedies.

I see how different childhood we all had

and how differently we all grew,

it leaves no space of second guess, I guess,

for why this world has 7.9 billion shades

we all never knew!

But, the irony is my EARTH MATE,

"Whatever you'll think the world has to offer you, it will offer you with no adulteration."

If you think the world is full of
pain and misery,
all that you will come across is
pain and misery.

If you think world is full of
magic and miracles,
all that you'll witness around you is
magic and miracles.

And if you think world is a mystery,
all that you'll see is mystery in even simple of
the simplest things possible too.

And it is so since what you believe is possible,

becomes possible for you.

If you think it exists, it exists
and if you don't, it doesn't.
If you think its possible, its possible
and if you don't, it never will.

With hope in eyes,
One shade of world from
7.9 billion shades of world,
Kanchan Pramod

LETTER - 2

(Amidst the empty)

"*This world, my love*
is so much more than you know,
there's is so much more in it to owe
and so much more you can't simply let go.
And this world, my love
has been so since ages ago.

It hides so much more than you think exists
and has so much unnoticed
in its every small bits.
It has got innumerable mysteries unresolved,
and infinite powers never evolved.

There still exists
thousands of places never visited
and hundreds of elements
touching whom is prohibited.

This world, my love, is a black hole,

you can get lost in it's darkness

for never to return again

and this world at the same time, my love,

is like that hidden island

of joy and treasure,

you can ask anything from

without any measure!"

Dear EARTH MATES,

This world will offer you everything you'll demand from it provided you are capable to handle whatever you are demanding for. And you become capable by trying everything possible to make yourself worthy of it.

Now, in your opinions are you yourself worthy of everything you dream and everything you pray for?

If yes, great.
If no, journey of worthiness is waiting for you.

Failing and falling

and frightening yet fighting

are the only ways for

self lightening and brightening,

then why are you always hiding

by running away or riding,

trying best not to get caught,

at any cost,

Ohh don't you just get exhaust?

Prove your desire for your dreams.

Fight for them.
Stand for them.
And most importantly work for them.

Your dreams turning into reality should never
be a surprise for you,
and if it is then you yourself did not believed in
your own efforts!

With hope in eyes,
One shade of world from
7.9 billion shades of world,
Kanchan Pramod

LETTER - 3

(WHAT do you BREATHE FOR ?)

"There is so much I can't erase
and so much I can't face,
so much to put back at its place
and so much for there is no space.

There are things I want
but can't trace
and things I like
but can't embrace.

There's a lot to love
and a lot worth a gaze,
now what to abandon
And what to chase?
Since my heart,
you can't travel both the ways!

I'm dying to fly with the fairies

somewhere high in the sky

but also dive with the mermaids

anywhere deeper in the see!

Ohh honey, that's the irony

I can't want it to rain

but also be sunny.

Still one day,

I wish to do it all

and say it aloud

not fear being amidst the crowd

but also love living alone on the cloud.

Ohh my fantasies…,

There is no way

for them all to be possible

But no great saint either said

For them all to be impossible."

Dear EARTH MATES,

If I ask you what do you breathe for, what is that one thing you want more and more desperately with every passing day, what would it be?

You may have got a list ready with you by now like having a fat bank balance, growing old with the love of your life, travelling to some unseen places and so on.

> *Some of these things may not*
>
> *make sense to others*
>
> *and some may seem*
>
> *meaningless to you yourself.*
>
> *Some of them may look*
>
> *impossible to achieve*
>
> *and some may seem*
>
> *very ordinary to be craved for.*

But I tell you my EARTH MATE,
it's all okay, as long as it's okay with you.

Even if it's just a tree you want to plant and watch it grow every single day,
Or you want to earn yourself a name and enjoy worldwide fame,
in either case, you don't have to explain anyone why it is so important for you.

> *I ask to none*
>
> *for what I want, I want*
>
> *And if I ask*
>
> *I see them ready*
>
> *with questions to haunt*
>
> *and judgements to taunt!*

Ask no questions when you see them ready with the answer you don't need.

**"I won't ask, I won't receive
and if I receive, I won't accept"** is the mantra of not seeking validation from society.

The day you truly accept others opinions don't matter, you will stop caring about those.

In your heart you know, what you thought about a person, about a situation and about everything rest.
You and only you know what good and bad you have prayed for people.
And it's only you who know what exactly your intentions were irrespective of the outcome.

So I believe, you are your own truth.

You don't need to prove anything to anyone, you don't need to make anyone believe in your good intentions and you absolutely don't need anyone to tell you what wrong or right you are doing, because in your heart you already know it all.

**Deep down in our hearts, we all know
what we are and what role we are playing!**

Whatever be the reason you are living for,
let no one tell you it's stupid or worthless
or right or wrong.
It's the cause you live for and it can never be
anything else but the reason you can die for.

Every person has

different reason to live,

some live for family

some breathe for love

some dream of wealth

and some fantasize life's depth!

If you live to give your parents a better life, cheers my EARTH MATE, it's a beautiful cause of living.

If you live for yourself, and take the responsibility of your own happiness and dreams, then double cheers my friend, it too is a beautiful cause of living.

And if there is anything else you live for, it will equally be beautiful since you breathe because of it.

Something for which I exist,

I am still in search of it,

Ordinary or astonishing

but I give no one the right

to tell me worth of it !

The purpose of one's life is never big or small, It's fulfilled and unfulfilled.

"Live life like a lost wanderer, enjoying and praising everything that comes your way,"

Since what you can see today,

may disappear tomorrow,

what you can touch today

may not exist tomorrow,

what you can feel today

may fade tomorrow

and what you call yours today

may become someone else's tomorrow.

Appreciate it all today

since regretting tomorrow

shall have nothing else to offer but sorrow!

You can dare to dream dreams contradicting to each other.
You can want to climb the mountains but also dive deep in the sea,
you can want to go fast but also go slow when tired,
And you can love yourself as you are but still want to work for your betterment.

It's all okay as long as you do it for yourself and not to satisfy or impress someone else.

Sometimes I wish to be everywhere like air

and witness everything fair and unfair,

the other times I wish to become invisible

for there's nothing I see is worth my care!

There are things we can't have but we still want,
And I find nothing wrong in it.
I find nothing wrong in trying to win what we can't afford to lose.
And I find absolutely nothing wrong at all in chasing something which gives us the zest to live.

What I feel to not be right is assuming failures in head, guessing negative outcomes without even actually trying and then finally not even giving it a try taking all those negative thoughts into consideration.

Like come on man, your dreams, your wishes, your desires are at least worth one try.
They are at least worth one failure and worth one bounce back.
They deserve one chance, even if it's the first and the last one.

They are at least of this much value, aren't they?

Whenever you question why some things
are happening to you,
remind yourself your wish
of what you want to be,
maybe whatever is happening to you
is the bridge between you
and the you which you want to be!

With hope in eyes,
One shade of world from
7.9 billion shades of world,
Kanchan Pramod

LETTER - 4

(Are Fantasies true?)

"*Depth of sea*
to the doors of heaven,
rages of hell
to the wonders all seven
I explore all,
every now and then
in hope to see the magic
which I read in class one.

I wish to see the secrets of fairies
and witness the existence of angels,
I desire to be the part of wild fantasies
and long to heal the wounds of strangers.
I crave the secrets of death wells
and lust for the beauty of magic spells,
I'm dying to know
the mystery of worlds running in parallel
and starve to witness the mystical ground
of stars which never fell.

Ohh I'm dead curious to know

how this world works

and freak to discover

do the feelings exist in the corpse?

I do everything it takes

to get me into that hidden den

and seek for the clues

in the words of the wise men.

I crave the secret of our grave

And unearth the phenomenon

causing the ocean wave!

Yes, I am a freak who seek

the magic behind life

and the reason behind death,

the emotions behind tears

and the feeling right before the last breathe!"

Dear EARTH MATES,

The world in our imagination is so confined, we only believe in the existence of what we can see through our naked eyes or can touch by our bare hands.

But who knows if fantasies are true,

Who knows if there ever existed a phoenix or if he still exists somewhere we never knew.

And who to guarantee, the existence of mermaids is only limited to one's imagination of the blue.

Who to assure, heaven and hell exist nowhere but only in head.

And who to swear, life after death is just a fiction, no one knows but ask the dead.

There is so much more to the world that I and you would have never fantasised about,

Thousands of doors never opened

and millions of roads never walked,

innumerable miracles never chased

and infinite ideas never thought.

There still exist the battles never fought

and the culprits never caught,

the love that was lost

and the people burning in hell

to repay the cost.

And researches are still being done

on how this world actually begun,

how the time first started to run

and how did the sun first started to burn?

How exactly did the water

form its first reflection

and how on earth did the shadows

got their first complexion?

So much of what we see, we see through the
eyes of our ancestors and think about from the
opinions of our elders.
We don't dare to question
and they don't bother to answer.

If only someday our curiosity drives us to reveal
the mysteries of this mysterious world, we shall
see the the infiniteness of this seemingly finite
spectrum.
Only then we shall be able to see the invisible
and look beyond what makes sense to our
ordinary senses.

No one has been to the whole world, we all are
the natives of some part of it.
It makes me realise how huge the world is, and
how difficult it is to discover all its unseen and
unheard places.

The more I dig in deep,

the more I drown in deep.

The more I drown in deep,

the more I explore depth.

The more I explore depth,

the more I discover

how everything here is complex and corrupt.

The more I discover

how everything is complex and corrupt,

the more I drive

towards danger, damage and disrupt.

The more I drive

towards danger, damage and disrupt,

the more I find myself in disgust

and the more I develop distrust.

Being curious by nature, we have somehow always been interested in how this world works, especially the things we were said we need not know.

[Were you never curious to know why according to some religions, we can not leave a dead body alone till the rituals are performed?]

But now I see that
It's okay for us to not know everything,
and sometimes it's rather better for us to not know everything

Since,

> *Some truths are hard to digest*
> *and harder to forget,*
> *they feel like any age old debt*
> *but no option than to accept.*

Life is easier to live
with some truths hidden,
and some mysteries unresolved,
some incidents unrevealed
and matters uninvolved.

With hope in eyes,
One shade of world from
7.9 billion shades of world,
Kanchan Pramod

LETTER - 5

(You can dream till you can breathe)

"*The best in me has yet not come,*

the worst of the struggles

I have yet not overcome,

the best version of me

I have yet not become

and the best places

I have yet not visited

where grows the cherry plum.

How can I stop here,

leaving all my dreams dead and run,

and how do I stop here

in the middle of none?

How can I stop here

without shining brighter before the sun

Or how do I stop here

before having the real work done?

Challenges to use all my capabilities

I have yet not witnessed

And I'm yet to settle

what once made me stressed.

I have yet not confessed to some people how

having them makes me feel blessed

And I'm yet to fix

what once I messed.

How can I stop here

leaving all in hell,

And how do I stop here,

return back, tell stories of my failure

and later yell ?

How do I?"

Dear EARTH MATES,

At times waves of some millions of thoughts about how your end would eventually be like may hit all at once on the surface of the ocean of your emotions. Some of them will be as sweet and sober as dying any peaceful death with no pain, no screams, nothing, just you and the devil having some heartfelt conversations.

While the others may be quite scary and painful to imagine such as dying in any road accident, drowning in water, burning alive, or dying after a long battle with any non-curable disease.

But imagine when your thoughts get way too extra creative with the ideas of your last breathe and surprisingly, until this day you never really realised how creative you have been all through your life.

Regardless of how amazing terrible ideas of your death your thoughts may come up with, yet not a single one from all of those can scare you to the extent that one thought can scare you.

Any guesses of that thought?

That one mere thought of you dying
before being able to make your dreams
come true,
before being able to find your real worth,
before being able to fulfil
the real cause of your life
And at last dying before being able to
live your best days with your best people
at some of your best dream places.

This single thought posses the potential of freaking you out a thousand times more.

Because dreams are those final destinations which give us the cause of living.

They are like those guiding lights which give the directions to our lives just like those fireflies which show us the way when it's dark all around. And constant dreaming of those dreams is like that one thought of finding an oasis in the desert which keeps us going, no matter how hard it becomes to walk and how dry it becomes to breathe.

In the simplest words if one needs to understand what dreams actually are and what potential they have, then take a look at all the million dollar companies of this century. They were dreams of someone, a mere fantasy but today you yourself see their huge absoluteness.

For all who know what dreams are

and for all who haven't yet met this shining star,

our every breathe is borrowed for a purpose

and that purpose is our dream

we have named so far.

With our breathes so limited

and time strictly fixed,

we haven't got forever for anything

thence, a chance ain't picked at once is missed.

Your real dream lives somewhere within you, just like your soul, no matter where you are or where you are going, with whom you are and what you are doing.

Dream and soul

share the same address of residence,

the address of your body,

no independent existence of either I see

and if I see, I need to see twice

to be sure of what I see is not a lie

in this world full of lies!

But,
Dreams don't walk to you,
you pave your way to them!

Hence, if you ever find a person
trying to achieve the impossible
or reach what's endless,
investing all he has,
working out all he could
but still not getting success at it,
then do not pity him.
I repeat just do not.
Do not at all feel sorry for him.
Be rather sorry for yourself,
pity yourself,
since he has at least started,
he managed to take that tough "first step."
What about you?
Have you ever thought about it?
Have you started doing anything for the things
you think you are living for?
Any real step and not just plans?
Any roadmap?

[Remember, the one who starts and takes the first step may someday reach his destination but the one who never even starts remains stuck at the same place forever.]

"You can dream till you can breathe."

Read it twice and you'll get the message -
"It's never too late to dream".

Now read that phrase again for as many times
as it takes for you to also uncover the second
message - :

"you can only dream till you have the breaths."

And with the handful number of breaths we are
born with, we never know which one is the last.

And no matter what you start,

sad and bad days will be a part,

a major one,

but that's how things are meant to be,

that's how universe checks

your patience, determination and will,

And that's how the stars get assured

of how far you can go

for the things you just can't simply let go.

That's exactly how the creator

of this world makes sure

for every small of the smallest thing

to be at its right place,

in the hands of its right deserving owner.

Thus, never consider any hurdle in your life as the obstacle, believe it or not but ups and downs are just part of the process, the process of you becoming your dream version of you, and the process of your dreams turning into reality.

The risen can fall,

and the fallen can rise,

here winner is the one

who continues this battle of tries!

Never abort the dream of flying because of the fear of falling down.

But no road here is the straight one.

And surprisingly, majority of the hurdles in your way will be caused by your own mixed emotions and inner wars.
You may   want something real badly for this moment and at the very next moment you may feel it to be of no worth.
But it's all okay, it's all normal.

 Just give some time to yourself and figure out what you really want.
One day, one week, one month or one whole year, any amount of time is okay when you have true intentions to return and start your incredible journey of your dreams someday.

And that day when you'll finally get your emotions settled, you will realise more bigger storms are awaited to be settled.
And the first one will obviously be your own habit of **laziness and procrastination,** followed by **starting and the dilemma,** then finally dealing with **demotivation by people.**

With hope in eyes,
One shade of world from
7.9 billion shades of world,
Kanchan Pramod

LETTER - 6

(Your soul knows where it belongs)

I was all blue and grey,

questioning my aura,

doubting what I pray,

rebel against everything

I was meant to obey,

And run away from everywhere

I was meant to stay!

I was all gloomy colour's ray,

wishing to drop everything that weigh

And wanting to stop dreaming every dream

that had any price attached to pay!

I was waiting for every precious thing

to come easy,

just kept standing at the coast

with my eyes closed

in hope to magically cross the sea.

But now I feel,

all that I really wanted

was just to be busy being cheesy lazy,

roaming in my slothful life's desert

in search of any victory daisy!

Alas my soul, that's not how universe work!

That's not even an inch of how

dreams kiss the dreamer's forehead,

because darling, success never reaches

the hands of a living dead,

a dead whose heart still can beat

and whose lungs still can breathe,

But his body, his body hid the most

deadliest death beneath,

a dreamless soul and a desire less spirit

residing within a living body like a culprit

I am sorry my love,
But, the world does not belong to these living
deads.

Dear EARTH MATES,

There once lived a boy amazingly good at one work - procrastination, like most of us. He used to keep procrastinating his every work, every project and every daily chore till the time it was the due date or the day he can not finally further delay. He himself did not liked to do it and wanted to change this habit.

Every night he used to get an irresistible inner call to get off the bed, go to his table and start the work which he has been postponing from weeks. But every night he wouldn't respond to that call waiting for sun to rise, morning sunlight to spread its wings all over his body and then he shall get up early in the morning, start his perfect planned plans with perfect mornings.

Alas mornings like such never blessed his eyes and he never started, until the night he get off his bed and started doing it.

Your tomorrow of " I will do it tomorrow " shall never come but " tomorrow is the deadline", this tomorrow will surely come.

So start today,

start tomorrow

or start never.

Whatever be it,

your fate will depend

on your own choices, forever.

But remember,
"Tomorrow is a forever journey"

Just start and go after your soul

coz your soul already knows the way!

It knows where it belongs,

it knows for what it longs,

it knows all your dusks and dawns

And all your rights and wrongs!

Your soul is familiar with the deepness

of what seems shallow in you,

and is aware of your secret love

that you yourself never knew!

It believes in your dreams

And understands your extremes.

So just silently listen to your soul
and chase it.
Trust me, you won't ever regret doing it.

Remember ,

Your delay today can make you pay someday.

Sometimes the price of such past blunders be as
high as loosing everything you might have
earned till yet,
the other times it will just be in the form of one
lifetime regret like a scar too deep
or a star too far
but always close and bright enough to keep
reminding you of your past mistakes no matter
at whatsoever place of universe you hide.

That's why I say,

delay….the lesser it is, the better it is!

Start with **planning,**
Proceed towards **preparation**
And meanwhile do not forget to embrace
the beauty of **patience.**

With hope in eyes,
One shade of world from
7.9 billion shades of world,
Kanchan Pramod

LETTER - 6

(You have not got forever for anything)

"Dreams in your eyes won't come true
by your nightlong cries
or by following fireflies.
They need your sweat,
they need your sleep,
they need your efforts
and they need it all without any leap.

Dreams in your eyes won't come true
by running behind comforting lies
or without letting you face
several failed tries.
Because dreams in your eyes
demand all you can dare
when the entire world becomes unfair,
when even your shadow stops to care,
And when your darling guiding angels also
start to give you death stare.

Dreams in your eyes are dying to witness

how much pain for them you can bear

and how badly you can get scared

when your own soul gives you a feeling

of not being home but somewhere elsewhere.

Dreams in your eyes wish to catch a glimpse of

how do you find a way when you are all froze

and how do you tackle the the days

when a huge storm of setbacks life throws,

how do you keep moving ahead

when also the air starts to oppose

and how do you keep holding on

when the thorns start to grow

on even the petals of your rose."

And at last,

Dreams in your eyes are curious to unearth

how will you keep your dreams alive

when every single hope starts to feel empty,

and no help seems to arrive for another eternity.

when all your prayers go unheard,

and pain doesn't vanish

even after the wound is cured!

Because,

Dreams in your eyes

want to be double assured of

how high price you can pay

for making your dreams stay.

(Sorry, I forgot to mention, dreams do not come true by only dreaming until you are God's favourite and are gifted with supernatural powers of achieving everything you dream without even having to move a finger for it, but then again that's a whole different scenario to be discussed.)

Dear EARTH MATES,

From all the little I know about this world,
if you are ready to pass the test
and pay the price,
you are equipped to receive the best
and secure the prize.

The universe fulfils the desires of all,
provided the desires are pure and worked for,
have been craved and cried for.

But, if you are okay living without it, it shall
always be okay staying away from you!

Some people's whole life passes between
"I want to do it" ,
"I will do it" and
"I will be doing it from tomorrow"
But then...
Their tomorrow never came.
They never started.
And everything remained the same!

You have not got forever for anything.

There is always a due date after which efforts don't count, confessions don't matter and realisations don't alter a thing.

(And I hope you realise this before the due date.)

Every opportunity, every good news and every confession comes with a default expiry date.
The opportunities that you have today, you may never get tomorrow, you can get better opportunities than today, you can get badder opportunities than today but none of them can be same as today.
Since your own situation will not be same as today, your mental state will not be same as today, and hence you altogether will not be same as today.

Life gives you chances to take opportunities but those opportunities shall never give you another chance to grab them.

Your time will come,

It surely will,

but not without your efforts,

and not without you leaving your comforts,

not without you trying,

and not at all without your own wish of flying,

not without your determination of standing up

again and retrying.

and definitely not without you qualifying!

Yes EARTH MATE, your time surely will come

when you'll actually work to bring it

and when you'll really commit to get it.

Someday your time will come,

Someday your veins will stop feeling numb,

And on some special day

your heart will gather enough courage

to take a step ahead

without being anxious about the outcome!

At night we sometimes feel very unproductive after realising for the whole day we did nothing then lazily laying on couch, eating, sleeping and scrolling down the phone screen.

But the very next day, we somehow end up repeating these exact same things.

It's okay.

Just take a long breathe and don't think much. All that you will get by thinking is more to think.
Start today, start even if it is the smallest step. And you'll see at every next step there will be more to achieve. No doubt, there will be smaller achievements in the beginning but do not undervalue them since these smaller achievements are the ones which give us courage to go for the bigger ones.

World needs dreamers and doers
not dreamers and delayers. Remember.

Don't just blankly worry about your career,
also take its responsibility and be sincere.
Start working for it,
No not from next next day,
next week or next year,
start it right at this moment
like any ready to go warrior.
Here you are the one man army
and your career the war
make one plan, two plans or million more
but start before today what tastes sweet
tomorrow turns sour.

Common habits lead to common places.
It's that simple!

If you own the habit of scrolling through the social media till midnight, or keep chatting with your beloved for the rest of night, then where do you think these habits of yours are taking you?
It's really not that these habits would take you nowhere but they will lead you to a place crowded by the crowd your habits made you to belong.

There's nothing here to get astonished about. Your habits were the habits of majority of the youngsters and all of you will mostly end up at one place. You already know that. Right? And if not, then prove this wrong.

Prove yourself wrong for yourself.

You may have met so many people who screamed right on your face " Success is not easy today. There is a lot of competition, a lot more hurdles and a lot more ups and downs than there used to be some decades ago."

Do you believe it?

Look around at the people in your college or school or workplace. Observe them. What do you think they are doing? Are they putting any real efforts towards the goal they might have set for themselves? I can swear, majority of them are not.

Most of them are just like you, wasting time, postponing things whenever given a chance and just dreaming but taking absolutely no actions for the same.

In order to achieve your goals and fulfil your desires,
all that you have to do is simply practice some self control.
- be a little more disciplined.
- stop postponing things.
- stop scrolling phone screen for hours.
- and put a full stop at every time consuming habit which doesn't add any value to your life.

You will see almost half of your work will be already done and you will be ahead of many like you without even doing any extra.

[One day you'll leave this world and not even a single person will have any clue about your dreams, and about your life changing idea. Work towards your goals or let them die with you and get buried in your grave, accompanying you.]

We are humans

and we feel everything.

From love to hatred,

pain to pleasure,

science to magic,

and hope to being lost.

The list is endless
since everything includes everything.
It's just what we let dominate,
It's just what we let create our fate.

When something belongs to you, it will make its way to you but when you know you belong to something then you make your way to it!

With hope in eyes,
One shade of world from
7.9 billion shades of world,
Kanchan Pramod

LETTER - 8

(Painful to remember)

Doubting my birth,

counting my worth,

missing missed chances

blaming those circumstances,

regretting life decisions

rooting the cause of my blur vision!

How did I cage

all my goodness in prison

and effortlessly embraced

this devilish position?

How did I not know

I was walking the wrong path

but now who to save me

from my own wrath?

"Is there really no way to go back in time"

I screamed to the heaven

and reply came for real "stop there and you won't

go any further therein"

It continued "my pen can't erase

what it has already penned

but could surely write better things

for your future, my friend

provided you yourself bring

your wrongs deeds to an end."

I wanted to tell him

that I never wanted to do it

but in this world of excuses,

I realised,

mine was the same with some moonlit.

Dear EARTH MATES,

The past that we have, I and you, is not to mourn upon but to learn from.

And if blur visions of that past still bother you,

Maybe for an opportunity that you missed
or a relation that you messed,
any innocent crime that you commit
or the guilt of not being someone's perfect fit,

Anything that didn't worked out in the past was not meant to work out there and everything that seemed not so right in the past was to settle all the wrongs of the future.

Things that might have got you insulted in the past taught you how to get respected in the future and things that failed you in the past taught you how to win in the future.

For everything that made you feel smaller in the past taught you how to be a giant in the future and everything that made you feel less in the past taught you how to be enough in the future.

Since all the things
that make you wrong once
also teach you
how to not be that wrong again!

And if it's true that "past can not be changed " then equally true is "past itself is not constant."
This moment, this very moment is past for the exact next moment.
Why then to mourn upon what's painful to remember?
Why not rather create a past we can be happy about?

With hope in eyes,
One shade of world from
7.9 billion shades of world,
Kanchan Pramod

LETTER - 9

(Universe has its own ways to settle things)

"Earn me a name

buy me some fame

gift me a crown

and make me best in the town"

I often cried this to the universe

and in return it made things more worse

like a curse all reverse.

It placed chains when I asked for wings

and brought the draught

when I prayed for springs,

made me a slave

when I wished to be one of those mighty kings

and grew blisters in my fingers

when I admired the moonstone rings.

It took me a decade to learn,

Universe never serves

the exact things you ask for

but never forgets to equip you

with the raw materials you will need

to create what your heart craves for.

Universe has it's own ways to settle things

and reunite all broken strings.

It gives tsunamis as chances

to wash sins

and failure as opportunities

to turn losses into wins.

Universe never fights your fight

for you to become your own knight,

polite and bright

yet strong enough to rebel against anything

that's not right in front of your sight.

Dear EARTH MATES,

This universe isn't a hotel that you'll be served all that you will demand. It's rather a kitchen where you will be furnished with all the ingredients, now depends upon you what you cook, with how much efforts you cook and at what pace you cook.

The universe wants us all to be winners and equally supports all of us. Its then the matter of our choice and our actions supporting what we choose.

Winners are not those who are best,

but those who inspite being

stressed, depressed and half dead

still refuse to give up,

and double the efforts instead.

If you think you are capable of winning all those seven oceans or could withstand the biggest ever explosions, you may actually be capable of that.

But of what use it is when you never get out of your comfort zone and start.

There are thousands of people who are capable of being the boss but remain clerk for their entire life and there are some other thousands of people who are roaming jobless but own the talent more than that of top rankers in their field.
And it's all since they didn't start their dream journey.

**So today, if because of your procrastination you start it late,
then later, don't condemn your fate.**

I have heard people saying "if it is in my destiny, it will make its way to me."
How I ask ?
None of the non living things on our planet have grown legs to make their way to you, it will always has to be you to use your legs and reach them.

Even if something is in your destiny, I say, it can't come to you until you are worth it and you deserve it and have done something as such like creating the channel for that thing.

Take an instance of a man who is destined to win the poetry competition to be held in his town. But do you think he will be able to win it, if he never even decides to participate in it ?

Yes, he may be destined to win it but only when both the two conditions are applied which are, he must participate and he must be good enough.

There are some things that are already written in the lines of our palms, but there will always be conditions applied.

For the success doesn't come to a fool
And if it comes, never stays!

With hope in eyes,
One shade of world from
7.9 billion shades of world,
Kanchan Pramod

LETTER - 10

(Choice of seconds)

You will be one of a kind my friend

if you don't find

what's really going on in your own mind

and what in you is making you so confined.

If you don't keep

your thoughts awake and aligned,

you'll only leave a regretful past behind,

before it gets impossible to return,

see what makes you blind

and leave all that keeps you bind,

or else like those excuse seekers my friend,

you'll become one of a kind!

It would be unbearably painful

to see an unknown

on the throne you always wished to own,

you then may groan,

you then may moan,

but alas my friend,

for everything and everyone here is a stone,

nor could see what good deeds

you have sown

and neither could hear

how empathetic was your tone

because in the end my friend

all that matters is

who won the throne!

Dear EARTH MATES,

Help people without any expectations but also without getting yourself harmed.

Since,

Do good to a person
And only the person knows
But do them bad,
And the entire world knows

(Even if they deserved that bad)

No one here tells what they did to someone, but all shall narrate what someone else did to them.

Support people if support is all they need,
but do not forget you also have a battle of your
own waiting to be fought.
Since in the end,
no one shall remember your good deed if you
fail to succeed.

History remembers only those who won,

neither those who were deserving to win

and nor the ones who lost by a second.

It's as simple. It's as precise.

No one is concerned about what you have gone
through and what all you have lost,
how hard you fell and how hard was it for you
to stand again,
if in the end you fail to win
or if in the end you lose even if it is by one damn
second.

Here,
every second counts because sometimes when you lose, you don't lose by an hour or a day, you lose by a second!

It's the choice you make in seconds to postpone a work and enjoy this moment. It's a choice made in seconds to take break from studying and start scrolling down the phone screens.

And it's a choice made in seconds "NOT TODAY, I WILL DO IT TOMORROW!"

Hence, it will be a choice made in seconds that will not give you a second chance to live and will swallow you up all at once.

If your dream doesn't give you enough motivation to stand up from bed and start to work, stop even calling it a dream, it's just a wish.

Once you want something badly enough, you yourself will stop making excuses.

It's good to accept your flaws, really good, but considering your reckless attitude to be "that's how I am" attitude is not at all appreciable because your reckless, lazy and procrastinating attitude is not a flaw, it's a choice. It's not something which cannot be changed, it can be worked upon and be improved!

With hope in eyes,
One shade of world from
7.9 billion shades of world,
Kanchan Pramod

LETTER - 11

(Deserving owner of questions)

 My dear EARTH MATE,

do not stop as soon as it becomes

a little harder to chop.

You never know

how many missions flop

before catching a robber prior the rob,

no one knows but ask the cop,

ask the owner how easy was it

to open his own shop

and ask the employee how effortless was it

to get his dream job.

Ask the raindrop how tender was it

to fall on ground all the way from top

and ask the poor how painless was it

to be unable to buy his child a lollipop.

Ask these questions to the their right owners

and you'll get answers

of where you stood wrong,

where was the need of being wise

and not strong!

You will learn,

you can't reach hilltop in a single go,

midway you will slip, fall and bleed

from tip to toe,

you'll get different answers

from different body parts,

the moment real test starts.

Some may want you to quit,

some may whisper to give another try,

the others be still wondering

where are we and why?

Being loaded with leather

it's no tough to enjoy biting cold weather,

It's then no hard to go with the flow,

what's hard is being naked

yet dancing in the chilling snow!

Dear EARTH MATES,

Everything will seem easy until you start,
BUT the day you finally start, you'll also start to
lose hope, you will start to realise things are not
as simple as they seem from far.
And nothing really ever was this effortless
for if it was painless,
everyone would have done it.

But how many BILL GATE do you see?
Or how many J K ROWLING you know?

So yes,

**The journey leading to dreams won't be easy,
But it will be worth it.**

Be sincere in whatever you are doing even if you don't like it today. Do it sincerely even if you have some other future plans or leave it altogether.

You have absolutely no idea where life may take you.
Like take an example of students. There are many students around the globe who are not at all interested in the field they are pursuing their high school or graduation in. Some of them are passionate about singing, dancing, photography or poetry. And using this as an excuse, they pay the least of their attention to studies. They constantly keep dreaming of their brighter career in the desired field.

And it's not that everyone of them fails, some do pursue their dream career but what about the rest of them?

They struggle life long. Here comes the role of their education into picture. Sometimes, being able to earn living also feels costly. But imagine if they would have paid attention to their studies along with their passion. Their condition would have never been this worse.

Yes, they might still be struggling with following their passion but they wouldn't had to struggle in order to make their ends meet.

I hence repeat, if you are doing something (studies, job, business or any sport),
do it sincerely or leave it altogether And go do something which you can do sincerely.

Moreover, knowledge and skill never harm even when in little excess.

What is already in your destiny will for sure make its way to you anyway. Question is about those which are not present in the lines of your palms.

We all know path to success, it's just that we also know hurdles in that path. Even then we do not give up on success but we start to search alternatives of that difficult path. We then start to look for short cuts and that's exactly where we all miss it.

Know one thing, path to heaven and path to success is only one - HARD WORK and GOOD DEEDS.

And don't even think working smart will make it any easier coz smart work also needs hard work.

Knowing that you are walking the wrong path is also a good thing, you can at least work in the right direction to be on track again. There are exist people who are still struggling to find if the path they are walking and the footprints they are following are leading them to their destination or to some other faraway station.

If you do not love and respect yourself as you are then work hard to become the version of you whom you can love, respect and be proud of!

With hope in eyes
One shade of world from
7.9 billion shades of world,
Kanchan Pramod

LETTER - 12

(Foes in friend's attire)

No pearl or platinum

no ruby or emerald,

neither any gem

nor any sapphire,

I see nothing as such to admire,

no desire and none to inspire.

There came a time when I felt,

honesty is to hire

and lover is a liar.

Nothing to acquire,

and everyone to conspire,

all I saw was everything under fire

and everyone to be foe in friend's attire.

Dear EARTH MATES,

Sometimes all those deceptions and bitter incidents which apparently fail to break us externally, break us internally.

Those deceptions, the least they never fail to do is break our trust, from everything and everyone.

No matter how strong we turn into, somehow we always remain delicate and vulnerable deep within.

We start to doubt everything that we see and don't see, the philosophies of world and reason of our existence, the intentions of people and the feelings of our own self.

We get stuck at a state

covered by all confusions,

one after other we draw

some thousand conclusions.

We fail to differentiate

what's actual and what's an illusion.

At this time what we crave most is clarity,
clarity in thoughts
and clarity in actions
clarity in life
and clarity in emotions.

Huge confusions take time to solve,
darker stains take time to vanish,
bigger changes take time to adapt,
And larger problems take time to settle.
So no matter how messed up
things are for now,
an adequate amount of time
will make everything alright,
just give some time to time.

There is no failure if you don't try.
But there shall be no success without trying.
Choice is always yours.

With hope in eyes,
One shade of world from
7.9 billion shades of world,
Kanchan Pramod

LETTER - 13

(Fear and failure)

Someday when failure strikes
I'll willingly welcome it
considering it to be my fate,
no hate, no debate
just accept what's served in my plate.
But I swear to not drop my sword there
run away to reach nowhere
or become blind and play unfair.

I will prepare harder
and dare to risk everything again,
I will aim sharper
and see how much can hurt the pain.
I would return to where I lost my war,
put back my armour on
and finish what I left unfinished
the other dawn.

I always knew

and shall always know,

even my fate can't take

my end to be so devastate.

I'll rebel, I'll repel,

bring down the hell

and cut down all witches spell

but finally rise again from where I fell.

Dear EARTH MATES,

Accept failure with smile
then turn it into success with your grace.

**But if you ever feel it's easy to deal with fear
and failure then you don't exactly know how
fear and failure feel like.**

Then you yet do not know how hard fear of
rejection hits, and how devastating is the feeling
of not being good enough.
You are yet to experience how heartbreaking it
is to accept you do not have what it takes to do
something and you are yet to encounter how
traumatic it is to see your blood and sweat
dream shatter into pieces.

Fear hits different
when accompanied with failure,
Fear hits harder
when it is to be faced alone
and the fear hits intense
when there seems no possible way to cope!

Near a pond in my way,

I ponder over -

the practice

behind the perfect,

and the preparation

behind the prize.

the prayer

behind the poetry

and the pressure

behind the progress!

the painful past

behind the prisoner

and the point

behind the polite.

It's never any perfect plan to lead you to success, it's the perfect preparation.

It's not about how awesome plans you make, it's about how awesomely you execute them. Sometimes the not so good plans beat those so called best plans. It's just a matter of preparation, patience, dedication and consistency.

And no matter what you do,
chances of failure will always remain an inseparable part.
Doesn't matter how hard you try but you won't be able to separate it from your future nor from your heart.
Yet you can do one thing,
you can make hard work the ultimate art of your life and become such a devoted artist of this art that the size of failure becomes unnoticeable, like something when looked from miles apart.

How often do you imagine about your future?

How often do you think what if somehow you unluckily fail in your plans?

How often do you question what if you happen to live the worst imagined days of your life?

How often do terror runs down your spine by getting a mere thought of what if your dreams remained dreams forever and never turned into reality?

And how often do you assume what if you fail to offer even basic necessities of living to your family if not luxuries altogether ?

Insecurity in dreams is immensely important. It makes you realise what your soul is thirsty for is not at all an easy target to aim upon. And now that you have aimed it already, you also have to spare equal amount of efforts to achieve it.

Dear, negativity has its own importance.

Thinking about failure, finding ways to deal with it, and looking for chances to avoid it, matters as much as positivity matters to keep going.

Hence negativity is important because balance is important.

And it's okay to start even with the most stupid idea. Because some people's most stupid ideas are the one of the most successful ones today. After all, you never know if an idea is going to work or not until you try it.

You can laugh without actually laughing
and can cry without actually crying,
But you can never die without really dying
and can never succeed without really trying!

In the process of germination, when the seed tries to make its way through the earth's crust, what percentage of possibility does it has of not being stepped on and getting crushed?
But because of the fear of being stepped on, does that seed ever chose to never grow up?
No it doesn't. It dares to make its way and face the world how it is. And because it dares, its chances of surviving increase. But imagine what if it gets scared and chooses to stay inside forever. Will it then ever grow up into a tree?

There are things which carry risk with them, but what on this planet comes completely risk free?

NOTHING. ABSOLUTELY NOTHING.

When you sleep, the ceiling fan above you may unfortunately just happen to fall right on your head and booom, game over...took no risk yet died!
Simply walking on road, chopping veggies or even chit chatting on mobile phone, everything is risky in itself.

So when you are compelled to take risks no matter what, then what's the point in not taking a little bigger and better ones, ones that posses the potential to change your entire life!

What's then is the point

to hide in a room?

Is it to chase away the doom

or linger for gloom to bloom?

Whatever be it

but deeper is the depth of death

and when it follows, you'll have

Nowhere to go,

Nobody to look for,

Nothing to lose

And not a thing to adore.

I hence ask -

If death is unavoidable,

it's delay is unaffordable,

then why not leave its thoughts

and become emotionally stable?

What's then left to worry?

what's then is the hurry?

Nothing's too late,

nothing's too early

everything is exactly

when it fairly should be.

After knowing this truth why not
love and enjoy our life journey
with all its struggle
why then to waste time screaming
" DEATH IS THE TROUBLE "

With hope in eyes,
One shade of world from
7.9 billion shades of world,
Kanchan Pramod

LETTER - 14

(Because dreams are dreams)

And in different chambers of my heart

reside different dreams I dreamed for me!

All equally important

all equally opposite,

all equally hard a bit

but all equally harder to quit.

Praying for one to win

feels no less than like

committing any secret sin

and wishing for one to come true

feels like wishing for

others to vanish out of blue.

Permitting one dream to beat in my chest

feels more or less like cheating on the rest.

And letting one to survive

feels horrible like killing the others alive.

Now,

Which one to keep

which one to drive

from which to walk away

and to which to arrive?

Dear EARTH MATES,

There will come situations in life where you will have to choose, choose between your favourites, since you can't have them all.
Some of the things are so contradictory to each other that it becomes impossible to choose both of them at the same time.

Now I know why

people don't together dream for sea and sky

for the more deeper into the sea you dive

the more away from the sky you drive.

You may have a real hard time accepting that you will have to let go some of your dreams.

Because in the end dreams are dreams!

We try all the possible ways to keep all of our dreams and make them work in parallel.

But in case all your attempts go in vain,
then understand that,

You can not show mercy and cruelty

at the same time.

Just like you can not be both

the saint and sinner under this same sky.

Sometimes you will have to choose, and its okay. But please remember by choosing one dream, you are not at all cheating on rest of your dreams. You just don't have any option to choose all of them.

How do I deal with myself

my own stupid self,

the stubborn me,

the struggling me,

self doubting me,

the procrastinating me,

the sensitive me,

and the savage me?

How do I stop craving for something

which ain't mine

And how to stop pretending all the time

to be happy, perfect and fine?

How do I stop the feeling

of not being good enough,

And how do I stop myself

from treating myself rude and rough?

How do I not leave things for tomorrow

and tomorrow how do I not be in

grief, regret and sorrow?

How do I feel and not feel the pain

at the same time

and how do I convince myself

having a moment of weakness is not a crime?

For too many times, we figure the problem and also know its solution.

But sometimes,
Knowing the solution isn't the solution,
being willing and determined to implement it,
is the one.

Even when we all know the problem is our laziness, we still find it hard to not be lazy.

Even when we know the problem is our inconsistency, we still struggle to be consistent.

And even when we know all our bad habits and addictions, it takes forever for us to change them.

Not loving ourselves for who we are and not loving the way we are, are two different things.
We must love and respect our deeper sense of existence, of who we truly are from heart.
But at the same time, we must also be able to figure where we stand wrong, and constantly keep improving to become the better version of ourselves.

With hope in eyes,
One shade of world from
7.9 billion shades of world,
Kanchan Pramod

LETTER - 15

(You are your own TRUTH)

If one questions which is more necessary,

the moon or the sun?

I say none,

We aren't fond of moon

neither admire the sun,

we just love the job being done!

If we aren't dependent,

then who's the sun

who's the moon,

what's then late

and what's too soon?

If moon and sun no longer bear life on earth,

will they still be of the same worth?

Dear EARTH MATES,

In life, we are only thankful to the things till the time we need them or till the time they have something to serve us.

We need land to walk and sky to fly
ocean to swim and tears to cry!

Once we generate substitute of a thing, it then no longer remains of the same worth in our eyes, be it a person or any materialistic thing. Sun, moon, land, air and water have no substitutes as of yet and hence are so necessary for us.

But wait for the day when we will have their substitutes, and that day you see the level their value will drop down to.

Nothing forever holds the same position and value.

You are your own truth

You are your own trust

You are your own belief

And you are your own blessing.

Dear EARTH MATE,

You are magic for you

and a whole sparkling cluster of miracles.

Now tell me how does that matter

what other people think of you?

Some people hate you without you knowing,
and also some love you without you knowing.

But the thing is

you never know,

who is lover,

and who is hater

until you trust the one

and regret later.

You never know who is who

until the one you feel is true

kills not only your body

but your soul too.

Some people hate you without any valid reason
and some may love you again without any valid
reason. And you don't have to blame yourself
for either.

Everything on this planet comes with its companion pair but can never live together at the same time and at the same place.

When you focus on well wishers, you feel more encouraged but when you focus on backbitchers, you constantly live in the fear of getting betrayed.

When you focus on lovers, you feel more blessed but when you focus on haters, you continuously doubt yourself and feel troubled.

When you focus on friends, you feel rewarded but when you focus on enemies, you feel drained instead.

Where there are well wishers

there exist backbitchers too,

Where there are lovers

there exist haters too ,

Where there are friends

there exist enemies too,

Some things just doesn't come alone,

life depends where your focus gets blown.

You can choose from choices but not from responsibilities. And it is your responsibility to not stop by hearing what people think about you, your dreams and your plans.

Who to trust, who to not

where to go, where to not

which to choose, which to not

how to live, how to not

when to quit, when to not

and what is mine, what is not

are the biggest questions of our life.

We never know who to trust

until we have trusted the wrong,

and only know where to go

until we are already where we don't belong.

We never know which road to choose

until we find ourselves

standing miles away from our goal

and never really know how to live

until traumatic past tears our soul.

We never know when to quit

until we are already late

and I don't know why

we never know who is ours

until he is driven away by our fate!

So trust me,
trusting yourself
is the only trust worth your trust,
believing yourself
is the only belief worth your belief,
and loving yourself
is the only love worth your love!

With hope in eyes,
One shade of world from
7.9 billion shades of world,
Kanchan Pramod

LETTER - 16

(No one is yours or mine)

Some will depart,

Some will join,

In this journey of life

no one is yours or mine.

You be right or be wrong,

you be weak or stay strong,

there will be some people your side,

and so will be some your opposite side.

But at last no one is your side or my side

they all are their profit's side,

or if not profit then for sure

not their loss's side.

Dear EARTH MATES,

Someday if you launch a success party of yours, you'll see many faces you haven't seen before, not at least in your bad days for sure.

We all have these kind of people around us.
They are not our friends neither are our foes.

They are just those people who pretend to be yours in front of you and someone else's in front of someone else!
These people are neither your side nor someone else's side, they are always their profit's side and if not profit, then for sure not their loss's side.

"Some places remind some faces,
those gazes, those praises
and everything else we caged
in our past's closed pages.
A relation we thought
would last for ages,
ended with the first phase
of changing phases.

Do you ever tell someone your real future plans?
Do you always speak what really goes in your mind?
Do you reveal all your cards to anyone?

Be honest, you don't. Hence never think anyone is weaker than you, don't ever underestimate anyone. You never know what are their future plans, you don't know what actually is going in their head and you never really know what cards they have kept hidden.

"There will be times when we'll have

less pleasure and more pain,

we will hear

less appreciation and more complain

we will experience

less love and more to explain.

And at times like these best reply to critics is silence.

But make sure that,

tomorrow your success
should make them think again
of what all they thought today,
and what all they talked today.

No matter how rich you get
but peace you can't borrow
and your mess you can't sell.

With hope in eyes,
One shade of world from
7.9 billion shades of world,
Kanchan Pramod

LETTER - 17

(Are things really the way they are?)

Clouds in thunder

make me wonder,

are things really the way they are?

Are stars happy to stay so far?

We live, we believe,

we believe what world made us believe,

but what we believe, is it always worth believing?

Dear EARTH MATES,

How simple the world seems till we don't question its laws, till we keep quiet and stay happy being silent sufferers. Question it to discover what you don't know and it shall make you question all that you know.

Ask the universe, the reason behind death and balance comes as an answer.
I believe it sometimes for I have heard it since I first asked this question.
But I also doubt it sometimes since it was never universe itself to answer rather those multiple people with multiple theories.

I doubt if its for balance or they have no better answer,
I doubt if it's the truth or its their incompetence to save the world.

I accept the cons

and admire the pros,

I love the rose

and the thorns?

now I befriend those!

In my life whatever goes

failure, rejection, pain and gain

I let no one know and no one knows

I no longer oppose

I no longer suppose

my pain, like any secret

in my heart I dispose!

We expect people to be as per our expectations, when we ourselves aren't as per our own expectations.

Believe me, no one gets any extra

than what he worked for

And no one gets what he ain't

capable of handling for sure,

be it happiness, sadness, success or failure

it's all a matter of deeds and efforts,

Since, truth never comes by running away

from all that hurts.

Respect whatever someone else has today.

Never get jealous of

what they have and you don't,

you never know if they did what you won't.

Never think someone has

what he doesn't deserve,

in no one's plate

God serves any extra serve.

Birth is magic,

death is mystery,

running researches but no victory,

what happens when we close our eyes

for never to open again,

is it a boon or bane?

loss or gain

how is the feeling,

how much is the pain?

do we not respond

but hear them all call and cry our name?

I don't know if it's boon or bane

but nothing ever remains the same,

don't know if it's loss or gain for the person

but for sure its a loss for his lovers,

for them it was so uncertain,

don't know if its blessing or curse

or it's something more worse.

Its verse of universe

or what if its beautiful, heavenly and all reverse,

whatever it be, its perfect at once,

needs no rehearse..!

Are stories true,

do they become stars and watch you all through ?

one with good deeds lands in heaven

and the other with wrong deeds in hell for lesson?

And,

here's where our stories end,

in a mysterious way

and with wish of living one more day.

With hope in eyes,
One shade of world from
7.9 billion shades of world,
Kanchan Pramod